THE CORE

The Essential Things You Must Know to be a Network Marketing Success

BY GEORGE AND MEKENZE

LIMIRI

DEDICATION

This book is dedicated to all current network marketers and all those who may be investigating the industry. We wish you the best in your pursuit of time and financial freedom.

TABLE OF CONTENTS

INTRODUCTION

In this era, where information is so readily available and technology seems to advance faster than we can keep up, it sometimes seems that the whole world is shifting. "Out with the old, in with the new." Many of our methods for everyday living are falling away as they become outdated, including nearly every imaginable type of business. With advances in technology and the social media boom, we are also seeing many new arenas come of age. Among those, network marketing is one that has arrived at its "sweet spot," where technology, demand, and society are all ripe and ready to run with it! There has never been a more appropriate time for the industry to flourish, and is it ever! Industry professional Jim Rohn once said, "Network marketing is the big wave of the future, and it's taking the place of franchising, which requires too much capital for the average person." Well, Mr. Rohn was right, and the future he spoke of is happening right now.

Did you know that people used to think of franchising as a scam? That the very idea of owning a franchise was something people looked down on? Franchising is now accepted all over the globe! It's nearly impossible to drive more than a few blocks without coming across a franchised business. Like franchising, network marketing is heading into a bright future. In the next decade, the question won't be, why are you involved in network marketing? Instead it will be, which network marketing company are you aligned with?

Not only is the timing perfect for this industry to thrive, but the financial situations of most American families are begging for the opportunity that network marketing delivers! As the Washington Post's E.J. Dionne Jr. stated clearly in 2012,

> *"We should face the fact that most families these days cannot afford to have one parent stay home with the kids. This is not about 'lifestyle' or 'values.' This is an economic struggle highlighting yet again the*

social costs arising from decades of stagnating or declining wages and growing income inequality."

Network marketing is the solution that people are praying for! Having another stream of income is crucial for even the most basic of needs, and the confidence that comes from knowing your loved ones are provided for is a natural human desire. Sadly, as the years pass for those who refuse to see that times are changing, that confidence is being depleted. Only those who evolve survive.

Network marketing is becoming a beacon of hope for millions of individuals and families because of the endless evidence that life can indeed be abundant in both time and money. We no longer have to sacrifice one for the other. This industry works for those who have caught the vision, and the number of people who have done so is growing. Regardless of background, education, race, or social status, everyone is offered a fresh chance at success with network marketing. Anyone—and we do mean *anyone*—can succeed!

So, why doesn't everyone make it? If the opportunity is so great, why do people fail? Why do people quit? We'll discuss these topics and others throughout the pages of this book. We'll point out the red flags and toss out the hype so you can see this industry for what it really is. We have no agenda aside from illustrating the skills you need to succeed with network marketing. We hope that by the time you finish, you'll have the attitude required to overcome obstacles and build the large organization you're dreaming of. That is the purpose of the book: To get right down to *the core* of network marketing and what you must know to succeed.

Now, let's dive in.

CHAPTER 1

What exactly is network marketing?

Network marketing is a business model used by some companies to distribute products or services, by building massive channels through an extremely effective form of advertising—word-of-mouth marketing. People sharing with other people! Not only is this form of advertising more effective, but the customer experience is also greatly enhanced, because the people distributing the products can act as guides to ensure that each customer has the best experience possible. The customer gains valuable knowledge and support on an individual basis, which simply isn't possible in other forms of marketing. People who actively share a product or service are known as "distributors," and they are compensated directly by the company. Since these companies require no budget for advertising, they can pay distributors handsomely for their efforts!

Besides distributing products or services, what else do network marketers do?

Aside from selling products, distributors build their teams by recruiting other people into their organizations, people who desire to build their own businesses as independent distributors. This process is what makes network marketing thrive as a business model. There is only so much a person can do alone. In fact, it's impossible to build a successful network marketing business alone! With a team of highly motivated distributors, the sky is limit.

Why are network marketing products so special?

If you don't purchase goods or services through a network marketing company, you are missing out on true quality! Remember, these companies aren't forced to spend millions of dollars every year on advertising. This means they have lots of room in their budgets to pay for product development, high-quality ingredients, and endless amounts of research. Any product that you pull from a supermarket shelf will pale in comparison to those put out by the network marketing industry, whether it be makeup, skin care, protein shakes, or jewelry. You'll find only the best!

Has the industry always had a good reputation?

In the beginning, the industry was met with mounds of criticism and direct attacks from major corporations who didn't want competition in the market place. Also, distributors often offered poor representations of what network marketing is all about and the effort it truly requires. Derogatory phrases like "get rich quick" or "pyramid schemes" come from people who were misled by those who claimed to be professionals in the industry. Every industry takes time to perfect itself, and no industry is without error.

But you can be certain that network marketing is no longer on trial. This industry is thriving, and you are one decision away from thriving in it. It all begins with finding a company that aligns with you, a product or service that you can fall in love with, and a rock-solid belief in yourself!

CHAPTER 2

How did it begin?

Many people think that network marketing got its start with companies like AMWAY or Mary Kay. And while those companies are indeed legendary and did help pave the way for what the industry is today, the concept began way before that—thousands of years before! The history of network marketing goes back over two thousand years, rising—believe it or not—simultaneously with one of the world's major religions. Jesus Christ may be the founder of Christianity, but he was also the original network marketer. The Bible clearly describes the system he used for spreading his message of love and the vision he had for mankind after death. He didn't use billboards, radio commercials, or a storefront. *He used people!* People teaching and sharing with other people—network marketing in its truest form.

Not convinced? Let's look even further into this example.

In the Bible, we read that just before Christ began his ministry, he had to recruit twelve disciples to assist him with his "business" of bringing about salvation to mankind. He needed to recruit a stable group of men who were willing to go the distance with him in spreading his Gospel. As you begin your own recruiting process, you can take comfort from knowing that even Christ himself went through challenges! He had to travel great distances and face bitter tribulation to find the people who would be willing to follow him and believe in his mission.

It is also important to keep in mind that he recruited ordinary men, not the rich and powerful rulers of the time. He knew that he would need a humble group who were open and willing to learn new skills. They would need to believe in him and have a passion for sharing his message with the people they knew and loved, as well as those they met for the first time. Although they started out ordinary, what a powerful group of networkers they became! Jesus was a true businessman who successfully utilized networking to impact every corner of the earth, and it's an impact that still ripples on today!

Dr. Robert Neff of Dallas, Texas, compiled the following list of ways Christianity matches up with network marketing:

1. It is very unlikely you'll learn about it unless someone else invites you to see it.

2. You are shown something that initially sounds too good to be true.

3. You are given support for its validity, but mostly through personal stories, and hence your belief is based mostly on faith.

4. You are told that you must first believe before you can experience the incredible benefits.

5. You can measure your belief by the amount of good that goes on around you.

6. You are given a manual to guide you.

7. While you may not understand it at first, you are asked to be teachable and follow those who have already experienced what still lies ahead for you.

8. Along the way, you will encounter difficulties and you will need to ask for assistance.

9. When up, you're asked to help others beneath you; and when down, you're able to get help from above.

10. That assistance will be given in a form that will make you stronger and more self-sufficient.

11. You will not be perfect along the way, but as long as you believe, you will reach your destination.

12. You are asked to delay gratification your putting your own needs aside for the time being so you can help others first.

13. Providing this help will require dedication, persistence and Hard-work.

14. Do not fear people, but instead offer a hand to them even though many will say they do not need your help.

15. By surrounding yourself with other good people who also carry the same beliefs and commitments, you are protected from negatives that

can hurt you.

16. You are invited to come together on a regular

basis to renew your vision.

17. As a result, you will learn more about

yourself, about others, and about life.

18. In the end, you will have directly or indirectly

helped thousands of people to live better lives and

move on to a better place.

CHAPTER 3

What do I have to do to get started?

Starting a network marketing business is very easy and affordable. Like any other business, it requires an upfront investment, but instead of being so high that no average person could foot the bill, the startup cost is usually only around a few hundred dollars. This is usually a product sample kit and is all for your personal consumption.

The startup cost also usually includes everything you'll need to sell the product and run a fully functioning business. Some companies may require you to pay a monthly fee—for your personal website or for website hosting—but no matter the case, the monthly overhead to run a potential million-dollar business will be unbelievably affordable, even for the average person on an average income.

Don't be scared away by the thought of having to purchase large amounts of inventory. The industry has evolved, and that is mostly no longer the case thanks to advances in website capabilities.

Generally, you'll only be required to purchase a minimal amount that you'll easily consume during the month. Monthly reorders are what create stable, residual income in network marketing. This is where true financial freedom comes into play, so let this sink in. When customers find value in a consumable product that they use regularly, they'll likely reorder every month for the rest of their lives. Residual orders = residual income.

What type of people decide to become network marketers?

Network marketing won't appeal to everybody. People who look into this type of business are usually ones looking to start part-time, flexible businesses with the potential of earning a more than full-time income. Ninety percent of people who stick with network marketing for at least ten years become wildly wealthy. However, there must be a steady, consistent increase in skill, knowledge, and action during that ten-year time frame. Doing nothing but wishing for ten years won't bring about results. Time isn't the only variable for success in this business, but time matched with a solid work ethic is the "secret sauce" that everyone seems to be searching for.

How important is a company's compensation plan?

Your company's compensation plan can make or break you. Do your research before jumping in with a company. It's a good idea to always ask your recruiter to explain their company's compensation plan while you take notes. If they can't explain it to you clearly and easily in just a few minutes, it's more than likely too complicated. Complicated plans are hard to duplicate and therefore aren't suitable for building a large, sustainable business.

This is one of the most overlooked aspects when it comes to deciding which company to align yourself with. A good compensation plan ensures that distributors who work hard to move product and build large organizations are appropriately rewarded.

Four main types of compensation plans exist in the industry today: Breakaway, Unilevel, Matrix, and Binary.

Breakaway *"is one of the oldest compensation plans still in use today. The name comes from the fact that distributors will advance their rank within the company, earning a greater commission rate with each rank, until they reach a certain point. Then they 'break away' from their up-line and are no longer part of their up-line's organization."*

The Unilevel plan *"allows you to sponsor as many distributors as you like, and you must place all of them on your frontline. However, rather than advancing and breaking away, everyone is paid the same commission rates. That's where the term unilevel comes from—everyone is on the same level."*

A Matrix compensation plan *"operates much like a unilevel plan does, but with one main difference. Each distributor can only sponsor a certain number of frontline distributors. Any additional distributors must be placed further down in their organization—such as their second level—and placed under another distributor."*

Binary compensation plans *"are characterized by having two legs, and only two legs. This makes them very simple. Most binary comp plans will pay you commissions on your weak leg only—the smaller leg that has less volume. This keeps most people focused on building their weak leg, which is also known as the pay leg in a binary compensation plan."*

While some companies may stick strictly to one of these plans, others have combined more than one type to create hybrids. This is another reason to have the person trying to recruit you explain their company's plan.

If you were to ask distributors from different companies why their compensation plan is the best, they would all give good reasons why all the others are less desirable. In all honesty, you can find successful individuals in all the above compensation plans. Each has its own unique checks and balances. Which compensation plan you choose comes down to preference. Do your own research, and select the one that makes the most sense to you and how you operate.

But remember that each plan will take time and a solid work ethic. Without these, you'll fail no matter which plan you choose. There is no avoiding the work in net*work* marketing.

What is geometric progression of numbers in network marketing?

Albert Einstein presented the idea that the compounding—or geometric progression—of numbers is the eighth wonder of the world. And it's also exactly what takes place in network marketing. Dictionary.com defines a geometric progression of numbers as "a sequence of terms in which the ratio between any two successive terms is the same, as the progression 1, 3, 9, 27, 81 or 144, 12, 1,1/12, 1/144."

Each company's progression of numbers is unique, and taking the time to understand what exactly is going on within the structure of your company's pay plan will help you stay motivated until you win. Network marketing is a numbers game, and the game will become much more exciting as you delve deeper into understanding what makes it tick.

How long should I stick with this business?

No matter how many times you may be told that you will make quick, easy money in network marketing, you must know that you won't become a success story simply by showing up. Enrolling in your business is only the beginning. Network marketing isn't a lottery ticket, even though some people have been misled into believing otherwise. Network marketing is a profession, and it takes just as much work and dedication as every other profession out there. If you treat it like a hobby, it will pay you like one. If someone tries to convince you that their opportunity requires no work and that all you need to do is sign up and watch the money start rolling in, run far away! As we said before, there is no avoiding the work in net*work* marketing.

The time it will take for you to achieve success depends largely on how you define "success." It's different for everyone. Someone who only wants a few hundred dollars to help ease the stress of household bills will achieve that goal

in less time than someone who wants to become a million-

dollar annual earner. Be realistic with the time frame that you

set for achieving your goals. If you keep the hype to a

minimum and stay focused, there's no way you can fail!

CHAPTER 4

What do I really need to know to succeed at this?

The principles at the heart of network marketing success aren't as complex as you might think. We feel that we have honed in on the focal points you'll need to move forward in this business, and believe us when we say that we have sorted through a lot of hype and unnecessary detours in coming up with these four principles. Hopefully this guidance will save you some time and frustration in your pursuits.

1) Decide what you want.

This is the starting point, and there's no use trying to skip over it. How can you reach your destination if you don't have a clue what that destination is? It may seem obvious, but too many people haven't truly decided why they are doing this network marketing thing in the first place. You must know what *you* want—not what your up-line wants, not what your parents want, and not what the million-dollar earners in your company want. The only way you'll have enough stamina to survive is if you are fueling up every day with the excitement that comes from the vision you have for *your* life and *your* future! You'll never hit a target you're not aiming for. If you can conceive it and believe it, you can achieve it.

2) Decide what you want to give up.

Distractions are the major reason that people don't progress in this business. They come in many forms: wasting time hanging out with friends who bring you down, choosing to party instead of going to a life-changing company event, binge-watching your favorite show on Netflix, etc. Most people underestimate the daily things that come up and distract them from engaging in income-producing activities, but the little things are what add up to become big things.

But this idea can work for you if you work on making your daily habits productive ones. What should you be doing daily? Engage in activities that will build you up as a person, such as listening to positive recordings or podcasts, spending time studying your company's training materials, or reading books that will build your skill and confidence. These things will help you do what matters most—sharing your product with people! Your product isn't going to move itself now, is it?

3) Find a mentor.

Who wouldn't want to cut down the time it takes to build a substantial business? To do that, you'll need to find someone who has already done it, figure out what daily actions they took along the way, and then *do those things*! There's no better shortcut than to find someone you admire who is willing to truthfully share their story with you. Find out what they did wrong and what they did right, and then utilize your new awareness as you continue your own way. You should be able to avoid many failures and road blocks just by watching for them. The best mentors are always humble and giving people, which is a big reason they're so successful. They'll gladly share advice in the hopes that you succeed even more quickly than they did. Keep in mind that you shouldn't only look at the amount of money a person earns or their current company rank when choosing a mentor.

You want to pick someone who has not only reached success but who has also brought many people with them!

Look for someone who has helped other people with no network marketing experience become great leaders. A leader who can build other leaders is someone you want to follow. If they have helped other people get to "the top," they can absolutely help you, too. Steer clear of those individuals who are self-centered in their business building. They are more concerned with their personal gain and glory than with uplifting as many people as they can on their journey.

4) Plan your work, then work your plan.

This step is the missing link for most people in network marketing. Without a plan, you'll fail; it's as simple as that. Decide what daily actions you need to take, then take those actions. A business plan is your road map to success. If you don't have a motivating plan, this business won't work. There is a certain subtlety to action planning, and it all centers around inner guidance and personal inspiration. Successful people are in tune with themselves and their individual flows. There are dozens of books and resources to help guide you when it comes to this important side of success. We don't have the space to cover them in this book, but we will say that you should keep your action plan flexible. Follow the daily inspiration that you receive and change your plan as you go. Do what feels right to you. If it feels forced, you're probably going in the wrong direction. There's no need to "re-invent the wheel" or overcomplicate. Keep it simple, but don't confuse simplicity with laziness.

CHAPTER 5

What behaviors do I need to develop to succeed?

In Merriam-Webster's collegiate dictionary, *behavior* is defined as "the manner of conducting oneself" or "anything that an organism does involving action and response to stimulation."

Success in network marketing requires a specific set of daily actions. Just like an aspiring NBA star must practice his jump shot every day, networkers must also develop certain skills—or behaviors—until they become second nature. Through our personal experience, we've found the following three behaviors to be of the utmost importance.

1) Preparation

There is a lot to learn about your company, products, compensation plan, and the countless other nuances that go along with your business. Don't get overwhelmed thinking that you have to learn every single detail before you can move forward. This is a "learn while you earn" business. You don't cram in information before an exam like in school.

27

Rather, you spend a little time in "preparation mode" on a regular basis. Learn a little more and become a little better every day.

Now the nice thing is that you won't have to purchase and study giant books or manuals because learning what you need to know in network marketing is just so darn easy! Most companies offer instant, on-line training tools that are easily accessible through their websites, YouTube channels, and other free, easy-to-use resources.

Be a good student of this industry, and commit to doing your own research regularly. Make it a part of your daily or weekly routine. Proper preparation makes the second behavior that much easier.

2) Presentation

I think we can agree that learning facts and gathering information is pointless until we begin sharing it with others, and this is what we call "presenting." The very essence of building your business is sharing what you learn with other people. Becoming good at this is what lets network marketers get paid the "big bucks."

Presenting is more than just standing in front of a crowd with a PowerPoint slideshow. A successful presentation happens anytime you can clearly relay the information you have to another person so that they understand and are equipped to make an informed decision whether what you're offering is the right fit for them. This can be done in so many ways, and so very easily! Companies normally create their own videos and tools to explain what they're all about, which makes it easier for the distributor to introduce the product or service to people. This opens the door for questions and dialogue between you and your prospect where you can give them the remaining information they need to begin their journey with the company. Network marketing presentations have literally become as simple as sharing a video or website from your smartphone, but no technology will ever replace your knowledge and ability to connect with your prospects on a human level. Technology is a great tool, but it won't do the whole job for you.

Preparing regularly and presenting effectively will help you find motivation for the third behavior.

3) Persistence

Persistence is a tricky quality to master because it is totally tied to your emotions and your ability to handle them. Emotions can take you on a constant roller-coaster ride, and that's not something you want in business. You need a clear mind and a combination of logic and inspired thought to lead you to your goals. But you're also a human being, so how do you keep your raging emotions under control?

It's important to recognize that network marketing is a very emotional business. Why? The short answer is that it's a people-oriented business. When you deal with other human beings, you aren't just going to experience their good qualities. You'll also get the crazy, negative, doubting, skeptical, and insecure aspects, as well! Unless you're prepared to handle it, this could cause you to throw in the towel.

Many people who fail in network marketing resist and fight the emotions that come with building this type of business, eventually burning themselves out. There's no way to bypass this part of the business, but if you are aware of the emotional storms that are out there, you can be prepared for them. If you are properly prepared, there's nothing to fear!

You'll have people who catch the vision of financial freedom that you share, and others who won't. You'll have people who criticize and mock you because you doing something outside the norm messes with their ego. Some people will knock you down; others will build you up. You'll gain friends because of your constant positive outlook, and you'll lose friends who can't handle it. You'll deal with all of this and more, so come prepared. When needed, lean on the people who truly want you to succeed.

CHAPTER 6

Why do people fail in network marketing?

A common misconception among people who are uneducated about network marketing is that only very few people succeed. While it may be true that only a small percentage of people who start in this industry become big-money earners, that's true of other businesses, too. There is no type of business where everyone makes it to the top.

Take medical careers, for instance. How many students enroll in a university with the intent of going through all the hoops required to become an MD? Do these ambitious students wind up with their own medical practices, or even get accepted into medical school? Of course, not. But people don't think of embarking on a career in medicine as a scam, like they do with network marketing. This comes from a simple lack of understanding. The more people who become educated about the industry, the faster this ignorance will die off.

The other factor that contributes to this erroneous thinking is that the initial investment to join a network marketing company is very small—so small, in fact, that it leads people to believe that the work ethic and skill set required should also be very small. Don't be fooled into thinking this. As we said earlier, treat it like a real business, and it will pay you like a real business.

Another misconception that will lead to sure failure is thinking that you are going to recruit a handful of people— most of them relatives—and you'll be set for success. Someone who tells you that you won't need to spend much time or energy recruiting people is leading you astray. You'll need to contact thousands of people throughout the course of your network marketing career, and there's no way of avoiding it. Learn to love and embrace this part of the work because it is the lifeblood of what we do. If you're taking the time to read this book, then the concept of networking probably already appeals to you. Networking is all about engaging with people and learning how you can serve them. This is the core of what we do. Love it! Embrace it!

Another common reason for failure is that most people simply don't believe in themselves. It may sound cliché, but this is the cause of more failure than everything else combined. In most cases, self-belief is a learned trait. Some people are raised in homes where they can naturally pick up on abundant self-confidence, but for most of us, it takes time, awareness, and dedication to learn—just like everything else worth having in life. If you can truly develop an attitude where you know that you can accomplish whatever you put your mind to, you'll be a winner in network marketing. So much of what we do is fueled by the inner drive that comes from self-confidence. It's well worth your time to read or listen to materials that will help you build that confidence. Surround yourself with people who already have it, and you'll pick up on it as well.

CHAPTER 7

How do I know if this is the right profession for me?

Anyone who takes the time to research and really understand network marketing will see that it is one of the best ways to create wealth and stability in life, by far. If the idea of creating a legacy of wealth for your family appeals to you, then you are a perfect candidate for what network marketing offers.

Much of society is wired to look to a job and a paycheck for their security. This is one of the worst ways to earn money or to create financial freedom or stability. Most people still embrace this system only because it's what they've been taught by their parents and school teachers. You now know that there are more options out there!

Along with being an incredible way to build a financial legacy, network marketing provides a lifestyle to admire. This is one of the only industries that gives you more and more time freedom while also helping you attain financial success. Really think about the power of this! Most people with big incomes also have big headaches at the end of every day and almost no time freedom. CEO's, doctors, lawyers, brick-and-mortar business owners. These people are usually enslaved by their businesses while network marketers are out enjoying the beach, their families, or any part of the world they choose to be in without their business suffering in the least. In fact, their business has the potential to grow by leaps and bounds while they soak up the sunshine on a beach somewhere. Imagine that!

Knowing whether this is the right profession for you comes down to some basic, personal questions that you can ask yourself.

First, do you really, *really* want both time and financial freedom? If the answer is a resounding YES, then you are probably already certain that this is the industry for you.

However, if you don't feel that resounding certainty, don't count yourself out just yet. Network marketing is far from a "one size fits all" type of business. If building wealth isn't a priority for you but you would still love to bring in a little extra money to help with the bills, network marketing can be for you. If you would like to leave one of your part time jobs so you have more time to spend with your loved ones, network marketing can be for you. Even if you're just a faithful product user who has had significant results and loves to share your experience with others, then yes, network marketing can be for you! Don't hesitate to join this great industry just because you don't have the desire to "go to the top." There's room for everyone, players both big and small.

How successful can I really become in network marketing?

When you commit time to building your own network marketing business and to rising to the top of your company's compensation plan, you'll realize that your income will be the envy of nearly all highly skilled professionals. Doctors, lawyers, engineers, small business owners, and even CEOs of large businesses will look at your lifestyle in awe! Not only will your income be incredible, but the time freedom that we mentioned before will set you apart as someone who lives "the good life." This is the American

Dream that has been talked about throughout the generations—the ability to generate a massive residual income from anywhere in the world on your own time schedule. It sounds almost too good to be true, but hopefully by now you can see that it's a real phenomenon!

We've found that the people who succeed with network marketing are those who have given themselves a "financial reality check." Everyone should truly look at what they have going on in their lives, right now. What's your current method of making money? Is it enough to give you the lifestyle you want? Will it be enough ten years from now? How about twenty? Now, if you're not happy with the answers to those questions, you need to change the direction you're going. We know this seems obvious, but hardly anyone takes the time to truthfully look in the mirror and evaluate their financial reflections. They just let life carry them aimlessly from one thing to the next. But that's not how financial freedom or success of any kind is created. It doesn't happen by accident!

People who give themselves this reality check realize that they need to give network marketing an honest look. There's nothing else in the world like it!

How do I inspire others to join me?

Network marketing thrives on duplication. You can't do this alone, even if you wanted to. It's impossible. Duplication happens when other people realize that they want in their lives what you're creating with your business in yours. It will take persistence on your part, because people will only want to join you when they're certain that you're serious about succeeding. One sure way to lose trust with the people watching you is to jump around from company to company, chasing after every shiny thing you see. Find your company, get grounded, and be persistent. People are watching you, whether you like it or not. As people begin to see your vision and your team starts to form, you want the magic of duplication to take place.

Duplication happens in these areas:

• *Duplication of your Efforts.*

- *Duplication of your Behaviors.*

- *Duplication of your Attitudes.*

Your team will do what you *do*, not what you *tell them to do*. A true leader leads by example. Simply informing, notifying, watching, inspecting, hoping, and expecting your team to do the work that you aren't currently doing is a sure recipe for failure. If you aren't out there working, your team won't be either.

But if you're staying in action and doing all you can to lead by example and your team still isn't growing, the only solution is to recruit a new group of distributors. Find more people, people who will do what's required! Don't waste too much time trying to motivate. We've come to realize that people can't be motivated externally, or at least, not for very long. It should come from within. They must want it as badly for themselves as you want it for yourself. Those people are out there, and it's your job to recognize them when you meet them.

The most successful network marketers know for a fact that their personal financial freedom and security lies in their personal effort. Those who are extremely successful in this industry do what most are unwilling to do, and that is why they earn like most won't.

CHAPTER 8

What is the most important principle for success?

In the first years of our journey building a network marketing business, we realized that we needed a certain element to bring together all the skills and hands-on knowledge we were acquiring. We call this element "Be, Do, Have."

Chances are that you're not quite aware of it, so let us explain. In life, we often believe that we need to *have* certain conditions (money, complete time freedom, a certain relationship) to finally *do* something worthwhile (travel with family, build your dream home, invest in real estate), which will then help us *be* everything we have ever imagined (successful, loving, fulfilled, admired).

When we realized that this was the *exact opposite* of what we needed to be doing, we knew that we had tapped into something very powerful.

Here's the formula in its correct sequence:

Making the simple switch from *having* first to *being* first is quite life-altering and will bring unimaginable ease into all areas of your life, including your network marketing pursuits. As human beings, we are programmed to feel a certain way about our current situation, and until we receive a physical manifestation or other evidence contradicting that, we cannot and should not change our outlook. This habit keeps us stuck and invites frustration in all its forms. Remembering that who and how we are being is what creates the building blocks for what we want to achieve is the key. *Being* comes first!

Here are a few things you can do to put this into practice when it comes to your network marketing goals:

• *Take some time to think about your overall vision for your business. Imagine how you will feel when accomplishing it.*

• *Embody those feelings and emotions in your life now, as opposed to waiting for the physical manifestation to show up. It's not about pretending to feel excited and happy, but conjuring up the real emotion from within by imagining your desires.*

• *Once those good emotions are resonating within you, think and talk about the specific actions you might take. Don't be in a rush to implement your ideas. Sit with them for a while, and let the excitement around them increase. When you're ready to act, you'll know it! You'll have all the emotional stamina you need, and the idea of action will be exciting to you!*

• Practice. Practice. Practice. Don't expect

perfection, and don't worry about arriving at any sort

of destination. This is something that will develop and

evolve over the course of your entire life. Have fun

with it!

"We do not attract that which we want, but that which we are."

– James Allen.

CONCLUSION

Final Thoughts

We hope that from reading through the principles we have shared, you now feel more confident in your choice to pursue this rewarding profession. Network marketing truly is one of the most exciting businesses to be a part of in the world today! It allows you the time, flexibility, and income to live life to the fullest, and it all starts with deciding to use what you have learned here as a springboard into your own journey, where you will surely learn your own lessons and gain your own insights.

We believe in you and your ability to succeed in network marketing, and we wish you the very best. See you at the top!

ABOUT THE AUTHORS

George and Mekenze Limiri met in early 2012 and were married less than a year later. They now have three kids, ages three and under, who are the main reason behind their love for the network marketing industry, because it allows them to be a "full-time family."

George was born and raised in Eastern Kenya and came to the United States in 2005. Mekenze is from Southern Utah.

They have a serious passion for network marketing and the lifestyle that comes with it. They are constantly learning and refining the art of this business, and they love sharing what they learn along the way.

BIBLIOGRAPHY

Allen, James. *As a Man Thinketh*. CreateSpace, 2014.

Chiara, Michael. "What is Network Marketing?"

November 4, 2013.

http://networkmarketing021.weebly.com/essay.html

Dictionary.com. *Geometric progression*. Random House,

Inc. http://www.dictionary.com/browse/geometric-

progression (accessed: March 21, 2017).

Dionne Jr., E.J. "Two-Paycheck Couples Are Quickly

Becoming the Norm." *The Washington Post*. April

18, 2012.

https://www.washingtonpost.com/opinions/two-

paycheck-couples-are-quickly-becoming-the-

norm/2012/04/18/gIQALSzlRT_story.html

Pilzer, Paul Zane. *The Wellness Revolution*. Wiley, 2002:

167.

Wesdorp, Ben. *Successful MLM Tips*.

http://successfulmlmtips.com/network-marketing-compensation-plans/

Yarnell, Mark and Rene Reid Yarnell. *Your First Year in Network Marketing*. Prima Publishing, 1998: 72–73

www.ingramcontent.com/pod-product-compliance
Lightning Source LLC
Chambersburg PA
CBHW070408190526
45169CB00003B/1170